Suzuki
Note Reading for Violin
by Shinichi Suzuki

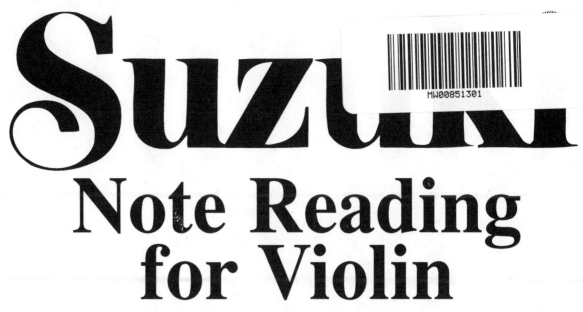

© 1956 Dr. Shinichi Suzuki
English Language Edition © 1985 Dr. Shinichi Suzuki
Sole publisher for the entire world except Japan:
Summy-Birchard Inc.
exclusively distributed by
Warner Bros. Publications
15800 N.W. 48th Avenue, Miami, Florida 33014
All rights reserved   Printed in U.S.A.

ISBN 0-87487-213-8

CONTENTS

This book is for children having difficulty due to a poor comprehension of written music for violin. Following the order of the Suzuki violin textbooks, this book will describe note reading, music theory, how to practice, and provide material that children should use to learn to play from music. I will be happy if this proves helpful to parents and children in solving those problems that arise during practice.

Part I
Open String Notes of the Violin

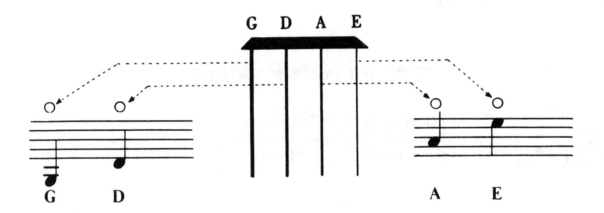

○ means an open string.

Lesson on Note Reading

Repeat each measure three times.

We do not use *do re mi fa* in practicing violin. Essential to performance is the ability to intuitively and quickly feel the notes and the sounds directly through the fingers. We teach the names of the notes after that. Note names are used only for open strings, for convenience's sake.

Reading Exercises
Twinkle to Perpetual Motion in A Major

Viewing the violin strings from above, the black dots show where the fingers should be placed.

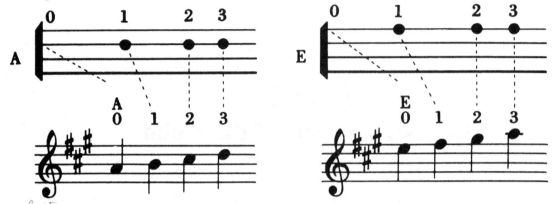

O indicates the open string. 1 means the forefinger, 2 the middle finger, and 3 the ring finger. (4 is the little finger.)

Lesson on Note Reading

The portion separated by vertical lines (bars) is called a measure.
When you practice, repeat each measure three times as you go.
I call this my Talent Education Method.

A String Exercises

This exercise involves the relationship between the notes and the fingers. Say the finger numbers as you read the notes, repeating each measure three times. With a precise rhythm in four beats, practice until you can do it correctly at a constant tempo.

Repeat each measure more than three times.

Lesson on the E String

In the exercise, clap out each beat as you say the finger numbers. Do it at a steady tempo. Always repeat each measure three times as you proceed.

Here you need not sing the melody. Train yourself until the finger numbers come to your lips intuitively.

Note Reading Practice

E and A Strings

Practice by repeating each measure three times as you proceed. Can you clap and say the finger numbers in tempo? Can you do it faster?

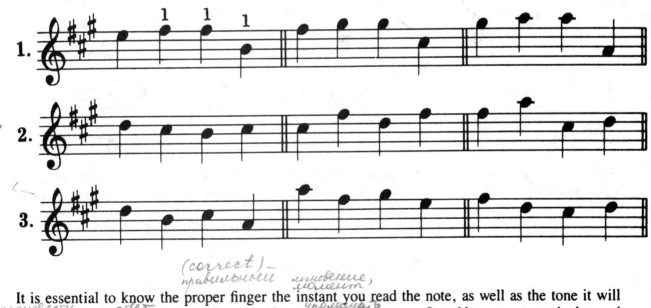

It is essential to know the proper finger the instant you read the note, as well as the tone it will produce. Your response will be too slow if you refer to note names first. Note names can be learned later to round out your musical knowledge. When the finger, the note, and the brain act as one, you know the tone the moment you read the note, as well as the melody. This talent education method is a new discovery. It corresponds to the relationship between words and letters. In language, children learn to speak first, before we teach them letters. I adopt the same process in teaching violin music.

If there are things you don't understand, please ask your teacher. I try to be as plain as possible, but it is sometimes difficult to explain everything in writing.

So far you have practiced saying the finger numbers (1,2,3) while glancing at the music. Perform the following exercise to test your ability thus far.

Sing the Melody and Fingers

Now practice saying the finger numbers while singing the melody of Lightly Row. Sing, for example, E 2 2, 3 1 1, . . .

If the rhythm of Lightly Row, above, gets muddled because finger numbers do not come quickly enough to your lips, you need to return to the previous exercises and practice them until your facility is more developed. In this way you will gain an intuitive grasp of notes and their corresponding finger numbers.

Song of the Wind

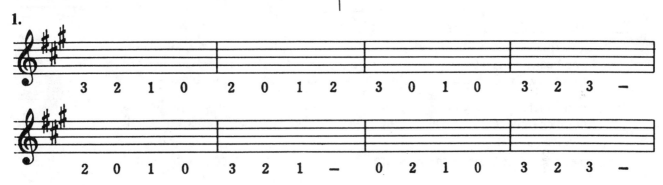

Go Tell Aunt Rhody

Writing in Notes on the E String

Next, practice writing in the notes that correspond to the finger numbers.

The dash means that the preceding note is held. Thus, 3- signifies finger number three is tied over for another quarter note value (making it a half note, ♩).

1.

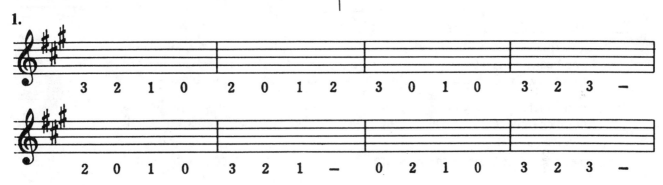

Practice until you can write in the notes in tempo, at the speed of one note for every two pulses.

2.

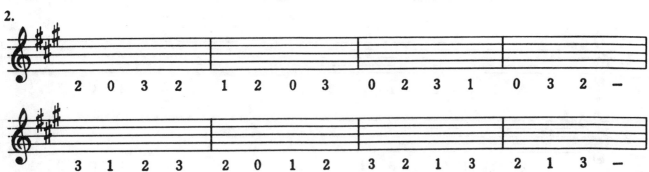

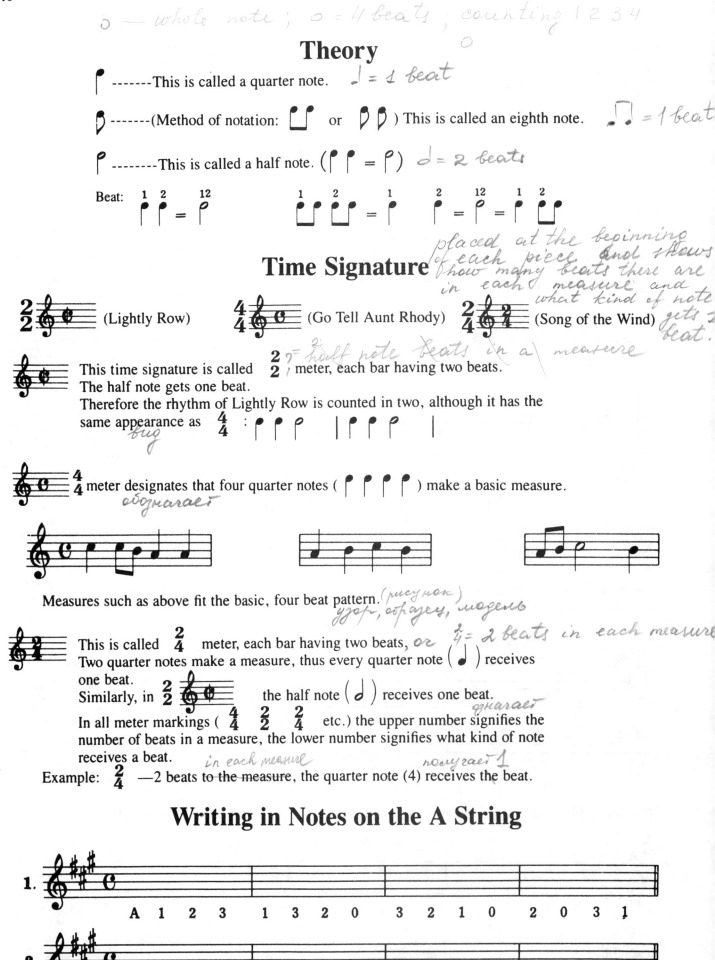

o — whole note ; o = 4 beats ; counting 1 2 3 4

Theory

♩ -------This is called a quarter note. *♩ = 1 beat*

♪ -------(Method of notation: ♫ or ♪ ♪) This is called an eighth note. *♫ = 1 beat*

♩ --------This is called a half note. (♩ ♩ = ♩) *♩ = 2 beats*

Beat: 1 2 12   1 2 1 2 12 1 2

Time Signature

placed at the beginning of each piece and shows how many beats there are in each measure and what kind of note gets 1 beat.

2/2 (Lightly Row)   **4/4** (Go Tell Aunt Rhody)   **2/4 2/4** (Song of the Wind)

2 = half note beats in a measure

This time signature is called **2/2** meter, each bar having two beats.
The half note gets one beat.
Therefore the rhythm of Lightly Row is counted in two, although it has the
same appearance as **4/4** : ♩ ♩ ♩ | ♩ ♩ ♩ |

bug

4/4 meter designates that four quarter notes (♩ ♩ ♩ ♩) make a basic measure.

обозначает

Measures such as above fit the basic, four beat pattern. *(рисунок)*
узор, образец, модель

This is called **2/4** meter, each bar having two beats, *or* *2/4 = 2 beats in each measure*
Two quarter notes make a measure, thus every quarter note (♩) receives
one beat.
Similarly, in **2/2** the half note (♩) receives one beat.
In all meter markings (**4/4** **2/2** **2/4** etc.) the upper number signifies the *значает*
number of beats in a measure, the lower number signifies what kind of note
receives a beat. *in each measure*   *получает 1*
Example: **2/4** —2 beats to the measure, the quarter note (4) receives the beat.

Writing in Notes on the A String

1.

A 1 2 3   1 3 2 0   3 2 1 0   2 0 3 1

2.

2 3 1 0   3 1 2 1   2 2 3 0   3 0 2 1

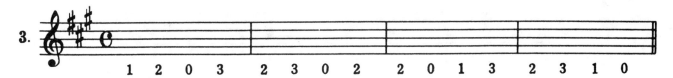

3.

1 2 0 3   2 3 0 2   2 0 1 3   2 3 1 0

Practice until you can write a note every two beats.

Writing in Notes on the A and E Strings

Write in notes:

1	0	3	2	3	0	1	2
E	E	E	E	A	A	A	A

3	2	3	2	1	3	3	1	2	3	2	3
A	A	E	E	E	E	A	A	E	A	A	E

Note Duration

продолжительность *длительность*

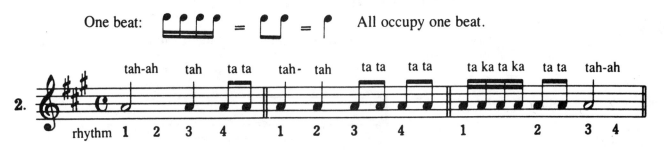

rhythm 1 2 3 4   1 2 3 4   1 2 3 4

Approach: One measure is in four beats. Practice while beating the rhythm with your hand. Watch so that the tempo of your hand-beating (four beats) does not change.

Sing the length of each note aloud, ta-ta-tah, ta-ta-tah, tah-ta-ta, etc.

One beat: **All occupy one beat.**

rhythm 1 2 3 4   1 2 3 4   1 2 3 4

If you find this difficult, practice the following first.

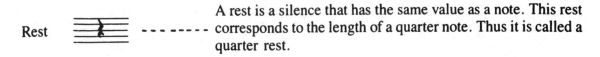

rhythm 1 2 3 4   rhythm 1 2 3 4   rhythm 1 2 3 4

Rest   - - - - - - - - A rest is a silence that has the same value as a note. This rest corresponds to the length of a quarter note. Thus it is called a quarter rest.

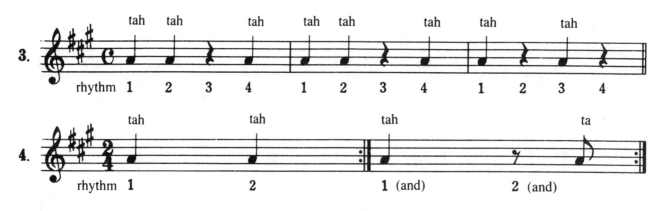

The eighth rest ⁷ - - - - This rest corresponds to the length of an eighth note, ♪

Rhythm and Note Duration

Write in the beats 1, 2, 3, 4 below.   An explanation below follows the dotted lines.

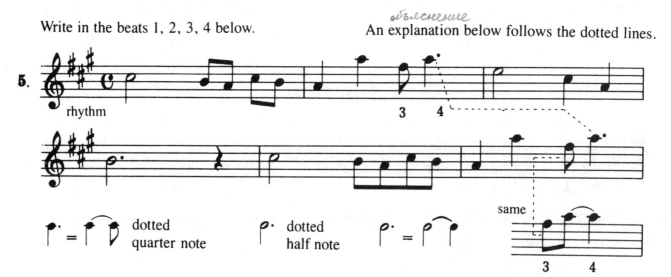

Lesson on the D String

In the case of the scale starting on D (D Major), too, the position of the fingers on the string is the same as in the cases of the A and E strings: 0 - 1 - 2 , 3 - (4 or 0).

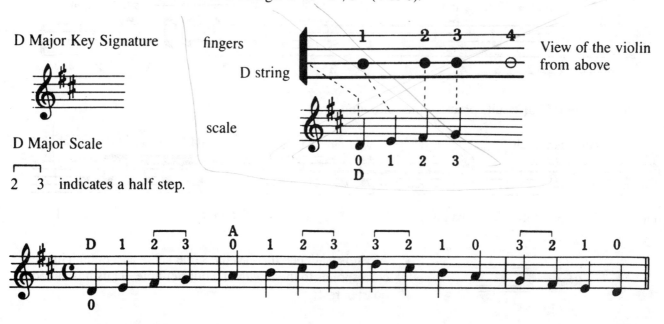

Lesson on Note Reading
D String

Practice reading finger numbers only without singing the melody. Repeat each measure three times in tempo.

A and D Strings

Say the finger numbers to the rhythm. If possible, sing the melody at the same time.

Holding the violin, practice placing your fingers intuitively, without sound. Repeat each measure three times.

D String

Practice so that you can gradually speed up the tempo.

A and D Strings

(Repeat each measure three times)

Talent Education

You will find that the more frequently you practice, the more ability you will acquire. It is alright to practice at a slow speed, but repeat it many times, with correct rhythm.

Lesson on Note Reading
G String

G Major Key Signature

The view of the violin from above

fingers

G string

scale

0   1   2   3   4

G 0   1   2   3

G Major Scale Over Two Strings
G and D

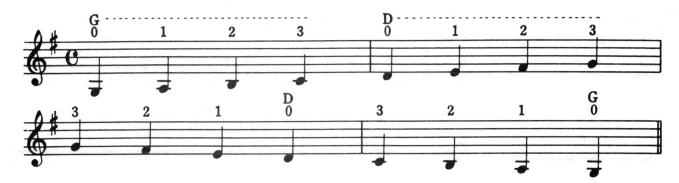

Reading Exercises

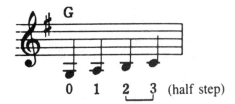

0   1   2   3   (half step)

Repeat each measure three times in tempo with precise rhythm.

1.

G string   Write in the notes:

2.

2   3   2   1   0   2   3   1   3   2   1   0   1   3   1   2

Exercises on Two Strings
G and D

Repeat each measure three times.

3.

4.

5.

Write in:

G - - - - - - D - - - - - - - - - - - G - - - - - - - - - - - - - - - - D - - - - - - - - - -
3   2   0   1   2   3   1   0   2   1   3   2   0   3   2   3

всесторонний, всеобъемлющий

Comprehensive Exercises

A and E strings

Repeat each measure three times, saying finger numbers 1, 2, 3.

Write in notes:

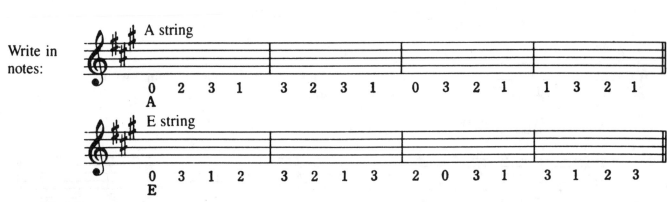

A string

| 0 | 2 | 3 | 1 | 3 | 2 | 3 | 1 | 0 | 3 | 2 | 1 | 1 | 3 | 2 | 1 |

A

E string

| 0 | 3 | 1 | 2 | 3 | 2 | 1 | 3 | 2 | 0 | 3 | 1 | 3 | 1 | 2 | 3 |

E

A and D strings

Repeat each measure three times.

Test your ability. Try the tempo a little faster.

D string

| 0 | 2 | 1 | 0 | 1 | 3 | 2 | 1 | 2 | 1 | 3 | 1 | 3 | 2 | 0 | 1 |

Write in:

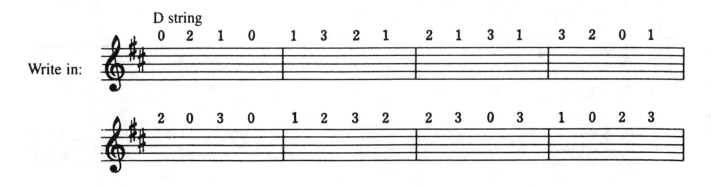

| 2 | 0 | 3 | 0 | 1 | 2 | 3 | 2 | 2 | 3 | 0 | 3 | 1 | 0 | 2 | 3 |

Practice until you can write one note every two beats.

Repeat each measure three times.

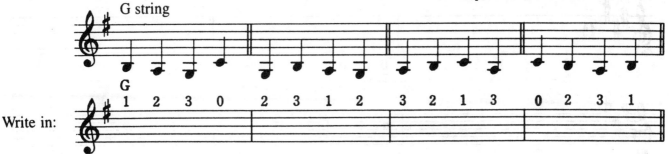

Time Signature

What are the following three time signatures? ($\frac{2}{4}$, $\frac{2}{2}$, or $\frac{4}{4}$).

A.

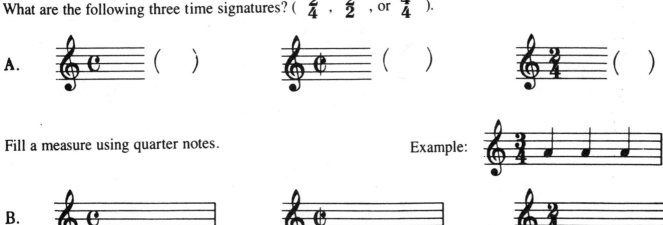

Fill a measure using quarter notes.   Example:

B.

Writing in Notes

The bracket over finger numbers indicates eighth notes (♪♪). As before, the dash (o–) shows that the note is tied over (o–= ♩♩ = ♩).

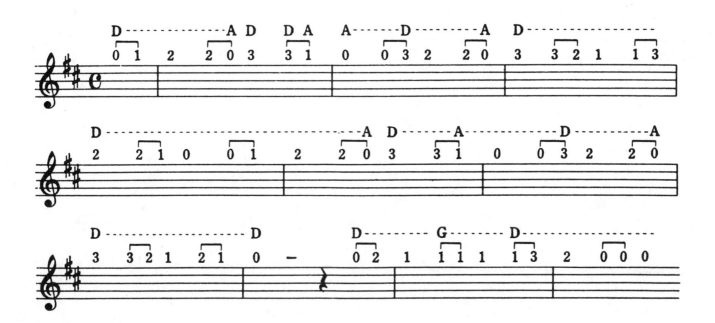

18

Part II

G Major Over the Four Strings

In Part I you practiced the finger positions for the G Major scale on the D and G strings. When you continue the G Major scale onto the A and E strings, moving to a higher octave, you must pull down the second finger so that it touches the first finger on both A and E strings.
Learn this finger pattern well.

The Position of the Second Finger
on the A String

The finger comes down half a step.
Put it close to the first finger.

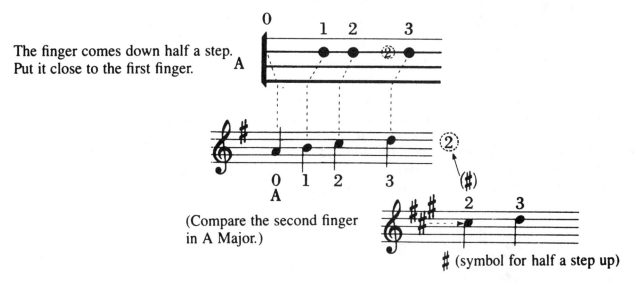

(Compare the second finger in A Major.)

♯ (symbol for half a step up)

Up until now, the second finger was half a step higher and you played it in a position next to the third finger. This time, put it next to the first finger (half a step lower).

The Position of the Second Finger
on the E String

Similarly put the second finger half a step lower close to the first finger.

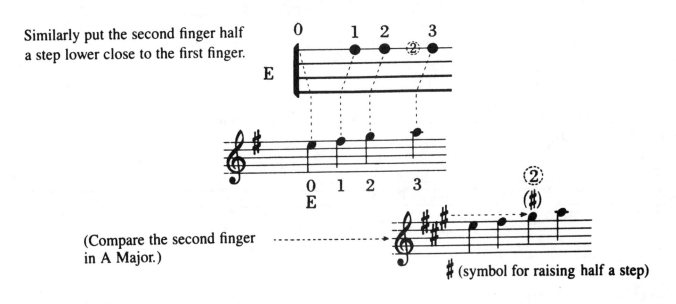

(Compare the second finger in A Major.)

♯ (symbol for raising half a step)

Finger Pattern of the G Major Scale
Over Four Strings

G Major

The sharp (♯) pertains to the same note regardless of octave.

The finger pattern for G Major, over all four strings, is as follows:

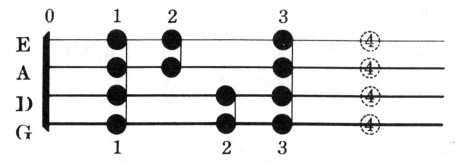

It is important to teach these finger patterns clearly to your child.

Those who strive to learn the precise intonation of the first and third fingers will have no trouble bringing the second finger half a step down, close to the third finger.

Those who have not learned the intonation of the first and third fingers will be imprecise in bringing the second finger close to the first. Those who have shaky intonation should first train themselves every day to correct the intonation of the first and third fingers.

The moment you see the music in G Major (one sharp), you have to think, "the second finger on A and E is close to first finger!!" (see the music above)

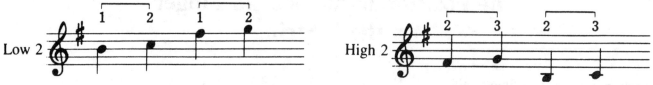

Then you must also know that the second finger on D and G is high, close to the third finger.

In the following exercise, look at the notes for the second finger and try to feel the position of that finger. Say aloud, "Low 2," "High 2," etc.

Now, look at the scale, and feel the position of the second finger; is it high 2, or low 2?

G Major

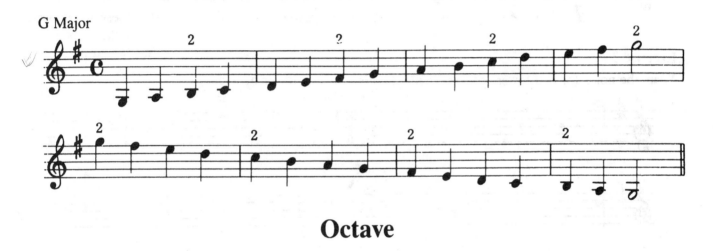

Octave

The first and last *do*'s in *do re mi fa sol la ti do* are the same sound one octave apart. It is the same when you use the note names A, B, C, etc.: one octave above A is A. The octave of G is G.

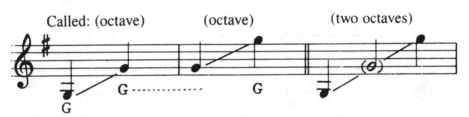

Here are the octaves in order:

Find the octaves and connect them with a pencil.

Example:

Exercise 1

Within each measure there is always a pair.

Exercise 2

Write an octave note for each note.

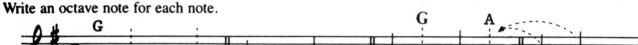

For these notes write two octave notes, one above and one below.

Exercise 3

Write the notes for two lower octaves. Write the note for one lower octave.

Names of Notes

Method 1) Read repeatedly. Read from the right also.

Method 2) After that, cover the letters and read from memory.

C Major

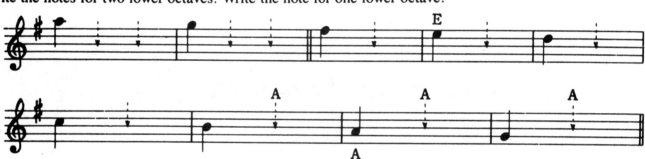

C D E F G A B C

C F B

There are only three notes which you are learning for the first time. You already know the rest: E, A, D, and G.

Learning Note Names

First practice in C Major.

Read each measure three times. Read octaves after you draw a line with a pencil.

Exercise 1

Even if you already know the notes, carefully repeat each measure three times every day looking
at the notes. The frequency of repetition creates ability.

Exercise 2

Repeat each measure three times.

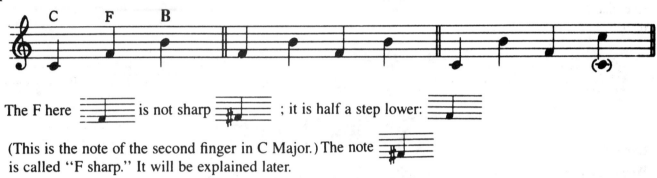

The F here ⎯⎯ is not sharp ⎯⎯ ; it is half a step lower: ⎯⎯

(This is the note of the second finger in C Major.) The note ⎯⎯
is called "F sharp." It will be explained later.

When you find octaves, draw a line between them with a pencil before you read them.

Exercise 3

Exercise 4

Even if you already know the material, please repeat for four or five days. That fosters ability.
When the above exercises are completed, go on to the practice of reading according to the beat.

Reading Exercise for Note Names
Song of the Wind

♪ = one pulse

C Major

Sharp

G Major  F sharp, F sharp, F sharp!!

Whether it is in the lower octave or the higher octave, it's F sharp, half a step higher than F natural.

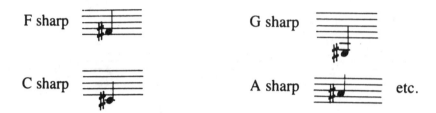

Reading in G Major

The one note in the G Major scale that differs from C Major is F sharp.

That's all!

G Major Scale Note Names

Repeat each measure three times.

Read each measure three times, repeating the note names, in tempo.

Finger Reading Exercises

Say fingers 1, 2, 3. Repeat each measure three times.
After that try reading all the way through.

Exercise 1
G Major

Try saying the note names.

Exercise 2

The Happy Farmer

Schumann

Exercise 3

Gavotte

Gossec

Exercise 4

Long, Long Ago

Exercise 5

rit - - - - -

Exercise 6

Repeat each measure three times.

Bourrée

Handel

Exercise 7

Lengths of Notes

To study the relationship between whole note, half note, quarter note, etc., and the beat, we will use a measure of four beats, in which the quarter note receives one beat. Recall that this is notated:

See examples below:

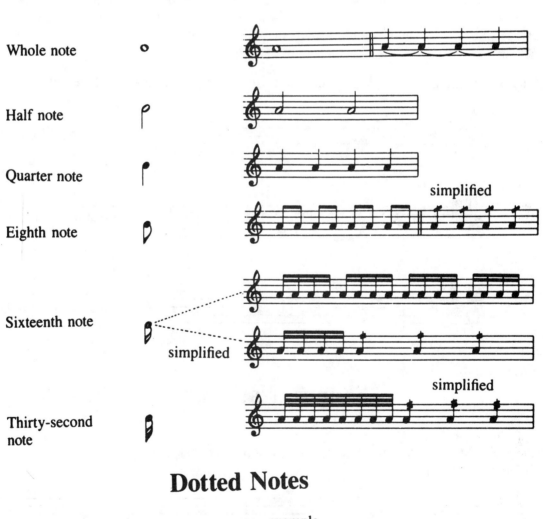

Whole note		
Half note		
Quarter note		
Eighth note		simplified
Sixteenth note		simplified
Thirty-second note		simplified

Dotted Notes

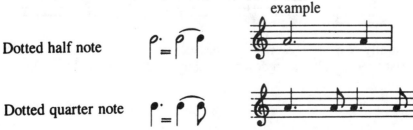

Dotted half note

Dotted quarter note

Dotted eighth note

Dotted sixteenth note

Avoid Illusions About the Lengths of Notes

Many people beat two times and stop, thinking that the half note (♩) counts as two beats. This is not long enough. A note receives its full value only when it is sustained through to the next beat. Try it. Only if you stop as you come to the third beat 1   2   3 , have you played the full length of the half note. (See the diagram.)

If you stop after 1, 2, you have played only the length of the quarter note (♩).
Hence, count until 4 for the dotted half note, ♩. ;
count five beats (1 2 3 4, 1), until the fifth beat for a whole note, o ;
and beat until 3 for the half note, ♩

Many people are misled in this. Be careful to sustain the final notes for their full values.

Stop at the third beat.

Stop at the fourth beat.

Stop at the second beat.

Sharps, Naturals, and Flats

Think of C Major as the fundamental key, with neither sharps nor flats.
All the notes are "natural": ♮

C Major

Think of it as the main family of notes. The rest are like members of branch families. When you restore a note which is flat (♭ , half a step down), or sharp (# , half a step up), you add a natural (♮) to the note.

A "flat" (♭) pulls the note down by a half step.
A "sharp" (♯) raises the note by a half step.
When a "natural" (♮) is attached, the note goes back to the main family.

Sharp (♯)

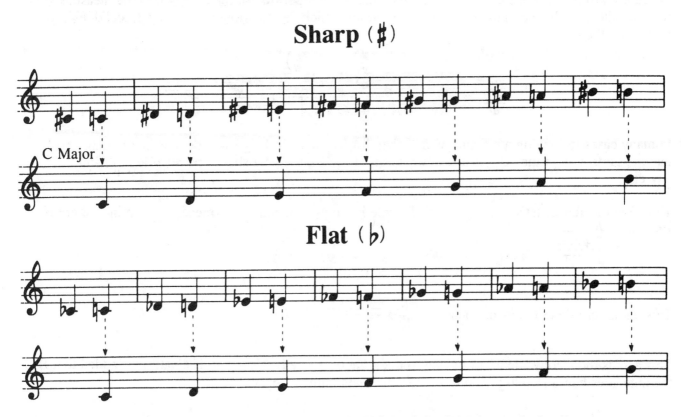

C Major

Flat (♭)

Only this occurs and nothing more. Try not to be misled. Think of the C Major, main family note when you see a note with a natural.

What happens when a note
with ♯ goes another half step higher,
or a note with ♭ goes another half
step lower?

For a double sharp, write ✗

For a double flat, write ♭♭

A — Returns to natural (main family) in one leap

B — Returns to one sharp

A — Back to natural (back to main family)

B — Returns to one flat

Sharps and Flats are Effective
Within the Same Measure

When a sharp or flat alters a note within a measure, each repetition of the note within the measure remains altered. This pertains only to the measure in which the notation is introduced, and does not carry over the bar.

In many cases, following a measure with a sharp or flat, a natural sign will be attached to make clear that the same note in the next measure is natural. However, the note should be regarded as natural in any case.

Knowing the above, let's study the Bach Double in Volume 4. Since this piece is in d minor, there is one flat:

This flat is for all the B's in any octave:

This avoids the inconvenience of having to put a flat on every B. However, if a natural is added to a B, the note goes half a step higher, returning to the main family, i.e., C Major:

C Major scale

Test yourself by writing in the finger numbers [0, 1, 2, 3, (high or low)].

This is from Volume 4, page 21, second staff from the top.

Natural, signalling a return home.

From the last measure of the fourth staff, page 21.

To make sure, here are main family notes once again:

Part III

Singing While Counting the Beat with Precision

Although one may know the time length of each note, one can acquire the ability to sing only by beating the rhythm correctly and giving the notes their correct length in time. This ability is indispensible; let me give examples for you to practice so that you can develop the skill.

For example, practice Long, Long Ago in different rhythms.
First, sing it counting a quarter note as one beat.

Long, Long Ago

Sing tah ta-ta etc., beating the rhythm with your hand.

Sing ta tah ta ta tah ta

(Syncopation)

This kind of rhythm is called syncopation.

Try singing tatta tatta

rhythm 1   2   3

*Think of this as groups of three plus two beats per measure (five beats total).

34

Practice differentiating between the sixteenth and eighth notes

------These are eighth notes.------

Exercise for rests

In the following, count an eighth note (♪) as one beat.

*The reason that I have marked the rhythm 1 (2,3) 2 (2,3), instead of 1, 2, 3, 4, 5, 6, is because this music (with 6/8 meter) is fundamentally divided into two beats.

Triplet

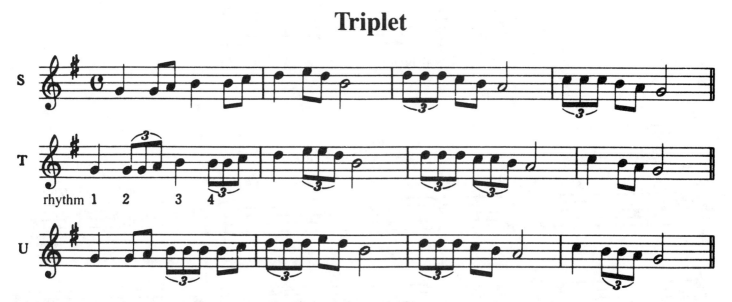

A triplet is a group of three notes that occupy a basic beat; in the above case, the basic beat has the value of a quarter note:

Reading Exercise
Low 1

From Volume 1 to this point, the first finger on the E string was always with a sharp, playing the position of high 1. In this piece, for the first time, low 1 appears.

Low 1 also appears in C Major scale, the main family of scales: 1 on E is low.

The Two Grenadiers is in d minor. The first finger on A and E is low.

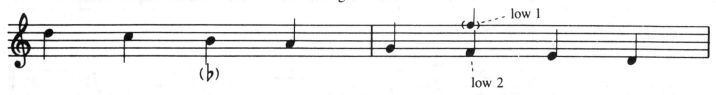

The second finger on D is also low.
Refer to the diagram below.

Finger Patterns in
The Two Grenadiers

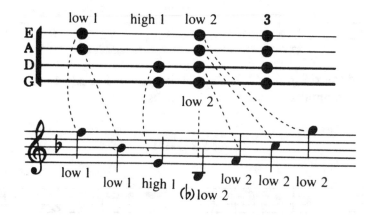

The Two Grenadiers

Moderato

Schumann

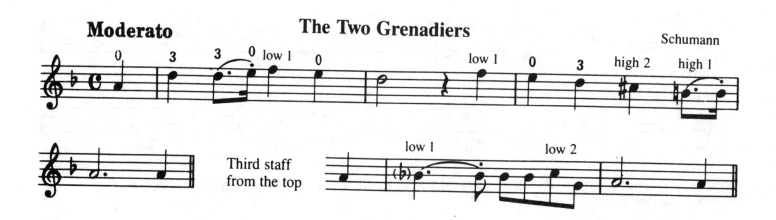

Third staff
from the top

Witches' Dance

Paganini

In Volume 2, finger patterns gradually begin to change. Those who have developed good intonation in G Major will understand changed finger positions. That is because the basics are there.
I have noted below, from the Gavotte from "Mignon," Volume 2, notes with sharps and flats in relation with the position of other fingers (4 touches 3, or 1 goes half a step lower). Compare and study.

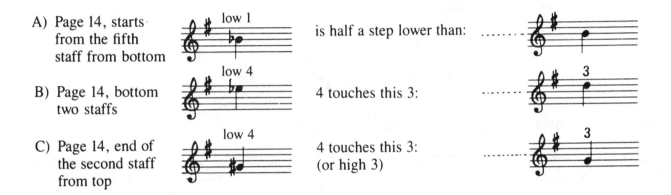

A) Page 14, starts from the fifth staff from bottom — is half a step lower than: ....

B) Page 14, bottom two staffs — 4 touches this 3: ....

C) Page 14, end of the second staff from top — 4 touches this 3: (or high 3)

Thus, you will learn the correct intonation of different tones in Volume 1, 2, and 3, as variations of 音程にと the basic tones of G Major.

My Idea
G Major and G Minor

Carefully look at Volumes 1 to 5.
You will notice that pieces in G Major and g minor have been consistently collected there.
Various changes in tone occur among them, generating other scales. The violin is made of four strings, G, D, A, and E, with the G string at the base. My idea is to train the student thoroughly in the basic scale of G, then to foster in him the ability to change to all the other scales with complete freedom. I think this idea has been successful.
Therefore, do your utmost to correctly grasp the intonation in G Major and g minor. This is essential for both parent and teacher.
Any ability that has been fostered to perform one task with excellence creates the judgement and intuition to handle other tasks. I have come to know this as one of the principles of human ability.
By fostering a student's efforts to become fluent in G Major and g minor, the student's strength is heightened. This is basic to my approach in editing the violin textbooks. When the ability is created to play the violin well, it becomes part of a person's human strength, and that strength is augmented in the functions of the brain. It is generally said that a man without a strong point is no good. That saying illustrates my principle.

Dynamics

When you watch your child's violin practice, pay careful attention to the bow length and musical expression. The following will be useful in this relation.

When increasing the volume, increase the bow length (long bow).
When decreasing the volume, use less bow length (short bow).

For lively and powerful sound, add speed to the bow.
When quiet sound is required, use a slow-moving bow.

The above variations are obvious to the eye; they are also obvious to the ear. Hence you will know it if you pay a little attention.

One who only uses long bows without reason;
One who only uses short bows without reason;
One who always uses the same bow speed:

Such a person has no dynamics in his tone.

Musical Dynamics

Take a measure, for example from Schumann's The Two Grenadiers:

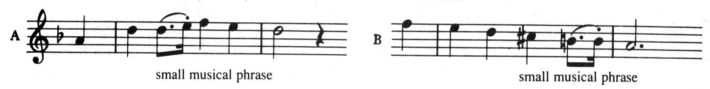

small musical phrase   small musical phrase

These are two small musical phrases. They are like two chains of words: In a sentence, we use commas after such phrases. It can be compared to something like: "When I went out to the yard early in the morning, beautiful flowers were in bloom." This sentence is broken into two sections, separated by a comma. Similarly, in music we phrase with the musical version of commas and periods. Thus we can express phrases clearly. In musical works, subordinate clauses separated by commas are called small phrases; together, they make up the large musical phrase, or passage, that ends with an unmistakable period.

Now concerning intonation within a small musical phrase, it is important to remember that, unless there is a specific indication of f (forte) or p (piano), dynamics should be added according to the variation of the pitch in sound.

Let's take The Two Grenadiers as an example.

dynamics

Take a careful look at the dynamic diagram indicated below the melody. Unless there is a special instruction, it is natural to express the dynamics of this piece as indicated in the diagram.

Minuet in G

Volume 2 (excerpt)

Beethoven

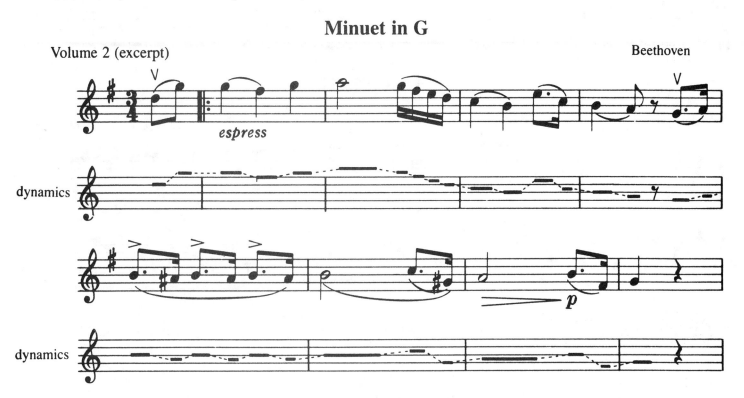

The appearance of the music is important in telling you how to feel the dynamics, and to sing the phrases through your instrument. The sight of the printed text signifies everything in determining musical character. A good facility for reading allows you to intuitively sense rhythm, phrasing, dynamics, and finger positions, as well as intonation, tempo, etc. In this book I have been gradually introducing these elements and providing exercises. With this understanding, please continue to read and practice the remainder of the book.

Reading Exercises

Test your ability. After practicing reading the finger numbers for the following excerpts, write in the finger numbers. (Write in high or low, too: high 2, low 4, etc.)

Gavotte from "Mignon"

Exercise 1 (Volume 2)

Thomas

10

Gavotte

Exercise 2 (Volume 2)

Lully

a minor

Minuet in G

Exercise 3 (Volume 2)

Beethoven

Gavotte

Exercise 4 (Volume 3)

Martini

Minuet

Exercise 5 (Volume 3)

Bach

g minor

Bach Minuet (Volume 3)

Becker Gavotte (Volume 3)

Study the following carefully for these pieces.

Two notes go down half a step when the key signature is two flats:

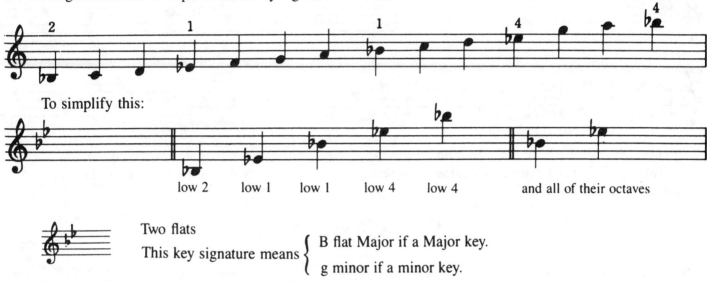

To simplify this:

low 2   low 1   low 1   low 4   low 4   and all of their octaves

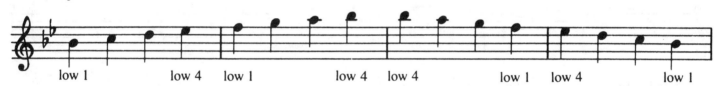

Two flats

This key signature means ⎧ B flat Major if a Major key.
⎩ g minor if a minor key.

B flat Major scale starts on B flat.

low 1   low 4   low 1   low 4   low 4   low 1   low 4   low 1

G minor scale starts on G.

G

Lesson on Reading
Low 1 and Low 4

First, read the following at the speed of a note for each pulse.

Minuet

Bach

This is an exercise in finding low 1 and low 4. Therefore, first look for the notes for low 4 and low 1. (There are seven.) Try quickly finding those seven. While you repeat this exercise, you will begin to understand the music.

Gavotte in G Minor

Bach

There are ten notes which are low 1 or low 4.
Practice finding them quickly. Repetition is a good practice.

When I see this note 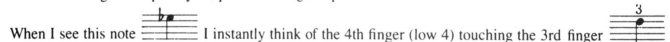 I instantly think of the 4th finger (low 4) touching the 3rd finger

Bourrée

Bach

There are fifteen low 4 or low 1 notes in the above.
Find them. Also try finding them starting from the bottom. Practice so that you reach 15 quickly.
When that is finished, proceed to practice in reading finger numbers.

Explanation of Keys

Take a careful look at the scale below:

Note names

Keys of

These are either called Major or minor depending upon the scale. In other words, C minor is a minor scale starting on C, and C Major is a Major scale starting on C.

If you learn the above clearly, the rest is simple: the key names change according to the first note of the scale. For example:

B flat ———— starts a B flat scale;   E flat ———— starts an E flat scale.

Exercise 4 Here is Twinkle in different keys.

The reason that the number of sharps and flats increase or decrease according to the key is because, as you play the scale from the first note of a key, high 3, high 2, low 4, etc. prove necessary. Instead of writing in ♯ or ♭ for each note, sharps and flats are all shown at the beginning as the key signature. This is an invention for convenience's sake.

In order to spare the trouble of adding a sharp to each note (A), a way to simplify this (B) was invented.

For the various keys above, write "high" or "low" before the numbers already printed ("high 2", "low 1", etc.).

Part IV

Table of Fingering Patterns
First Position

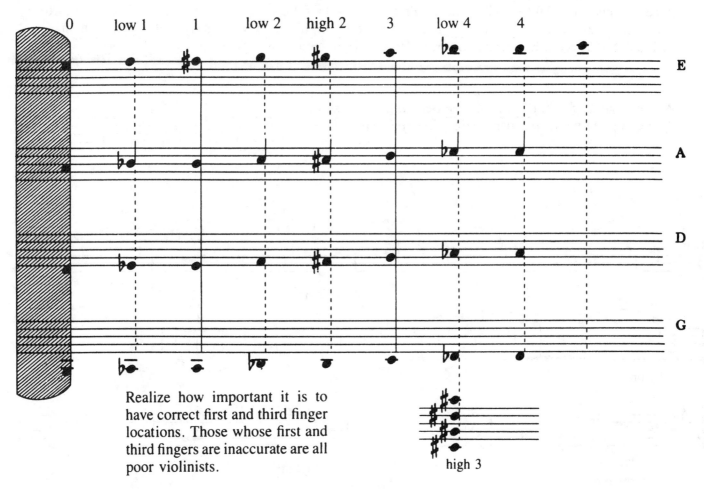

Realize how important it is to have correct first and third finger locations. Those whose first and third fingers are inaccurate are all poor violinists.

Conceptually speaking, you can help your child secure his finger positions most effectively when you place emphasis on the first and third fingers. Use the following terms.

You must train precise intonation and proper tone of the 1st and 3rd fingers. The sounds of these two fingers are basic.

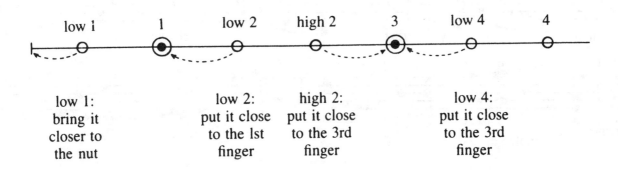

low 1:
bring it
closer to
the nut

low 2:
put it close
to the lst
finger

high 2:
put it close
to the 3rd
finger

low 4:
put it close
to the 3rd
finger

Please refer to the table of fingering patterns. The locations of the fingers are the same regardless of the string. I am sure you now understand how important it is to help your child develop the ability to produce accurate tone with the lst and 3rd fingers.

Low 2 is close to the 1st finger; high 2 is close to the 3rd finger; low 4 is close to the 3rd finger—it is necessary to repeat practicing until these expressions become part of the children's basic knowledge. Practice developing reliable intonation in the lst and 3rd fingers, even if it takes a long time.

This is my talent education approach.

The ability to carry the rhythm without becoming ruffled, the ability to clearly understand position of fingers—this is crucial to reading music. Practice well the following excerpts from the Seitz Concerto No. 5, first movement (Volume 4). If necessary, write "high" or "low" lightly with a pencil, then erase later. Practice it frequently. Go over the exercise mentally.

Where it says "rhythm" practice the beat in that measure.
Where you see numbers, mark "high" or "low" in red.

Exercise 1

Exercise 2

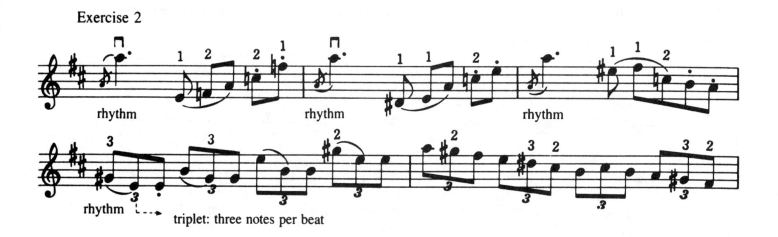

triplet: three notes per beat

Exercise 3

Reading Exercises

Where a half step occurs (where two fingers are close together), mark it with ⌐ as in and . The following are exercises for recognizing half steps with the eye, rather than with the ear.

48

Seitz Concerto No. 5
Third Movement

Look at the Seitz Concerto No. 5, 3rd Movement, and test yourself. With the ability you have accumulated, see how easily you can now understand finger patterns and rhythms.

The key is D Major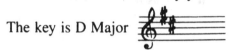

Mark half steps with ⌐ , think or say low 1, high 2, low 2, etc. Also practice reading finger numbers.

Rhythm Practice

Practice the following, beating the meter, 1, 2, 1, 2, etc. Sing each measure three times. Never allow yourself to rush.

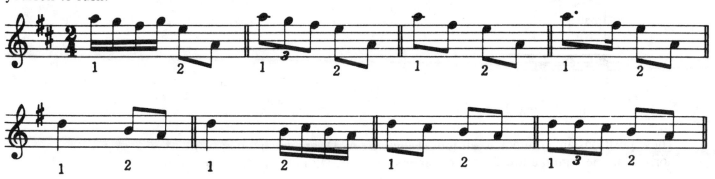

Rhythm is an important framework of music. Poor rhythm is a severe weakness in music.

Notes on the Seitz Concerto No. 5

See Volume 4, page 13, 4th staff from the top, 3rd measure. There is a section like this:

Take a look at the table of finger patterns. The positions for and are in a straight horizontal line.

In such a case, first put the 1st finger down on D, then slide it a little toward the G string so that it presses both of the 1st finger positions on D and G.
If you do that, you will find a spot where you can play both notes accurately.
You must not try to put your finger down first on G, or bring your finger between the two strings.
When you give your child a lesson, try not to forget this. Again, don't try to play the three strings all at once, but divide the three notes into and playing two strings at a time (4th measure, 5th staff from the top, page 13).

Reading in Finger Patterns

Read top and bottom notes separately

You must have accurate intonation of low 1 on D and low 2 on A *while pressing both notes*. Practice slowly, paying attention to *low 1 and low 2*.
When you play two strings together, what you must be careful about is precision of the finger position on each string. Refer to the table. I will discuss below how to create that ability.

Half step (fingers close together)   whole step (twice the space of half step)

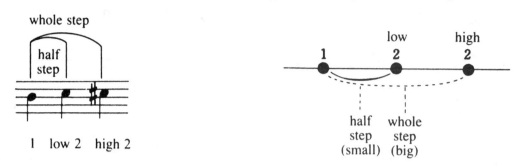

These positions are common to all four strings, E, A, D, and G. In other words, low 2 on A is in a horizontal line with the low 2's on the other strings, E, D, and G (refer to the table).

Finger positions, side view.

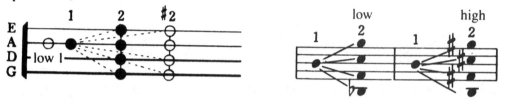

Big Space—Small Space

This is an important point in reading or in performing; read carefully, and ask your teacher if you don't understand.

Example:

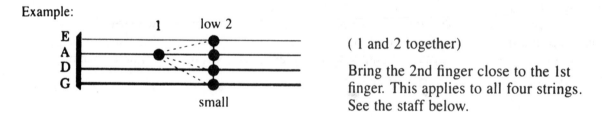

(1 and 2 together)

Bring the 2nd finger close to the 1st finger. This applies to all four strings. See the staff below.

Play without moving the 1st finger; the 2nd finger should be close to the 1st finger (all four strings):

Example:

Put 2 close to 1. I call this "small." Read the following.

When you see measures such as the following, you will intuitively think that 1 and 2 have to be together. Knowing that the distance between fingers is the same, even when the fingers rest on different strings, simplifies playing and reading. There is no need to grope around for positions. I call the half step "small," and the whole step "big" in explaining finger positions and relationships between fingers.

Small Finger Pattern—fingers together for "small."

1 and 2 together

"Small" space: keeping the first finger on, think about the location of low 2's.

I call this finger pattern "small." If you still don't understand it, refer to the finger pattern table.

When you come to clearly know the placement of fingers and their sound, violin becomes very easy both in reading and playing.

"Big" space—put the 2nd finger close to the 3rd finger for a whole step ("big") between 1 and 2.

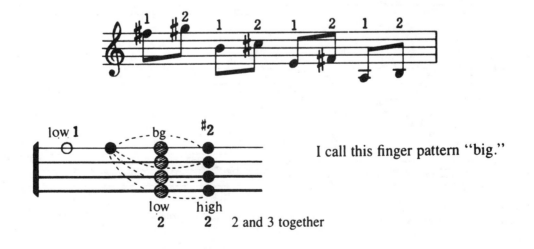

I call this finger pattern "big."

From the foregoing, you will understand that high 2 is always in the same position even if on a different string; it is in the same vertical distance on the fingerboard from the basic finger 1 or 3. Let me give some examples below.

Big finger pattern (1 and 2) Pretend that you don't move the 1st finger; then think about the location of the 2nd finger. In the following, the space between the two fingers is always "big."

The relationship between fingers can be understood as half steps or whole steps. Realize that the relationship remains the same even *if you shift a finger to another string*.

"Big" space (2 and 3)

With this knowledge, take another look at the double stops in the third movement of Seitz Concerto No. 5: you will understand the relationship between fingers fairly well now.

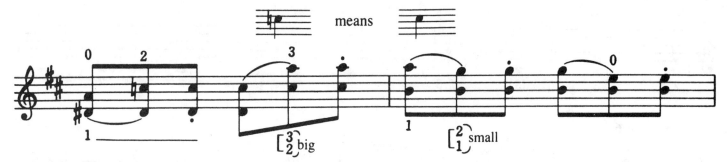

I will let you give further study to the question of finger spaces big and small with additional exercises.

Exercises in Distinguishing Between Big and Small

Concerto in A Minor

Exercise 1 (Volume 4)

Vivaldi

Write down big or small for all the fingers except for 3 3 in the middle; 3 2, 3 2, 1 2, and 2 3 at the end. Even if you are talking about a finger space over two different strings, you should still be able to show the finger relationship using big or small. Put a bracket ⌐ ¬ for a small space. Leave big as it is. This means that any of the first, second, third, and fourth fingers can have a big or small relationship with an adjacent finger according to it position. Realize that "small" applies not only to a half step between fingers on the same string, but to their relationship between fingers on different strings. "Big" is reckoned similarly.

Exercise 2

Mark big or small. Put ⌐ ¬ for small.   It is the same in the case of double stops.

Exercise 3

Repeat each measure more than three times; then mark.

Mark big or small.

Exercise 4

As you gradually understand "big" and "small," it will become clear when you should put your fingers together, or separate them.

Exercise 5

Exercise 6

Second Position

Around the time the student practices the Seitz concertos, the training in *Position Etudes* begins. It prepares the student to be able to securely play in the second and third positions by the time he starts lessons on Vivaldi.

Table of Fingering Patterns
Second Position

I give lessons to my students on the entire book of *Position Etudes* three times within two years or so. I think it is best to train the student to fluently play the book within two years.

Using the familiar 1st position as the basis, the 2nd position builds the finger pattern starting where the 1st position, 2nd finger was. In other words, in 2nd position, your 1st finger is placed where the 2nd finger would normally be in first position; 2nd is placed where third would be, etc.

Let's try playing a scale using the A and E Strings.

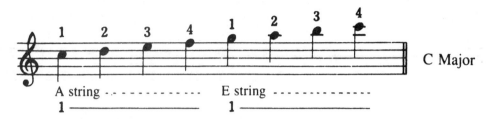

Keep the 1st finger down.

It is most important to foster intuition for positions.

Carefully examine the table of 2nd position finger patterns, then find the finger pattern of this scale.

Let's try playing a scale using G and D strings.

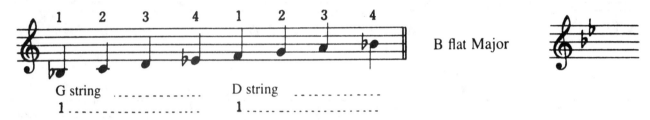

Let's try playing a scale using the D and A string.

Finger Reading Exercises
Second Position

Repeat each measure more than three times in reading the following.

No.1

Whether with a sharp or a flat, the finger is the same.

The following mixes the 1st and 2nd positions.

I indicates 1st position   II indicates 2nd position.

No..10

Concerto in A Minor
Third Movement

Read the fingers more than three times, then write in the finger numbers.

Vivaldi

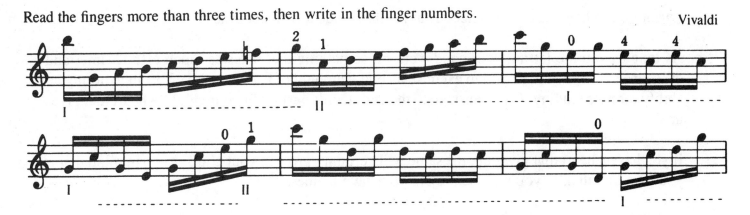

More Finger Reading Exercises

Where it is not marked in the 2nd position (II...) play in the 1st position. After reading the fingers three or four times carefully, write in the finger numbers.

Many people develop the ability to give up instantly when they can't do something upon first trial. "I'm no good," is what they think.

These people do not know themselves at all. That they cannot do it at present only means that they have not developed the ability. They have not tried, and practiced. That does not mean you "can't do it." What others can do, you can do as well.

Take time so that you will be able to do it, using the proper approach in practice, and repeat diligently, making every effort to foster your ability.

I want you to have this confidence. That is talent education's doctrine.

As long as you are letting your child work on something that takes as much effort, time, and diligence as violin, I want you to exercise an equal amount of patience and effort in fostering an ability for note reading. Carry through to the end. Don't nurture in your child "a heart that gives up."

If you have a heart that gives up, the same will certainly grow in your child. Keep in mind that if you give up quickly, you may be prey to your own laziness.

Steadily, slowly, patiently foster your own strength, and you will, in turn, foster violin playing ability.

Those who are anxious to advance their children to more difficult pieces, when real ability is not yet fostered (through lack of practice), simply chase their children into a hell of agony.

Be the kind of person who knows that one's ability develops only when one takes the time required for growth.

Part V

Musical Notes and Rhythm

quarter note . . . . one beat

half note . . . . two beats

dotted half note . . . . three beats

whole note . . . . four beats

E string (this is the slimmest string—Open string).
Below is an example of four beats.

Keep the correct rhythm as you play. This is the A string, next to the E string.

This is the D string, next to A.

This is the G string, next to D.

Quarter and eighth notes   Eighth

Eighth and sixteenth notes   Sixteenth

𝄿 eighth rest, equal in duration to ♪

𝄿 sixteenth rest, equal in duration to ♬

𝄿 thirty-second rest, equal in duration to ♬

𝄽 quarter rest, equal in duration to ♩

thirty-second note ♬ (𝅘𝅥𝅲𝅘𝅥𝅲𝅘𝅥𝅲𝅘𝅥𝅲 𝅘𝅥𝅲𝅘𝅥𝅲𝅘𝅥𝅲𝅘𝅥𝅲𝅘𝅥𝅲𝅘𝅥𝅲𝅘𝅥𝅲𝅘𝅥𝅲)

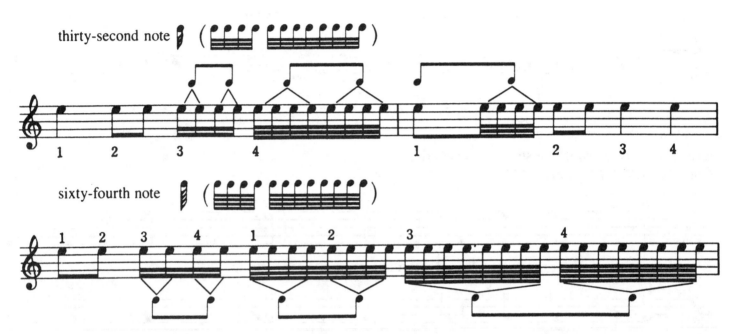

sixty-fourth note ♬ (𝅘𝅥𝅳𝅘𝅥𝅳𝅘𝅥𝅳𝅘𝅥𝅳 𝅘𝅥𝅳𝅘𝅥𝅳𝅘𝅥𝅳𝅘𝅥𝅳𝅘𝅥𝅳𝅘𝅥𝅳)

You will understand it well if you count ♪ as one beat.

Reading Exercises

Look at the music yourself and play while thinking carefully about the rhythm.

I am sure it will be pleasant when familiar and beautiful pieces flow out of the notes.

G Major

Repeat each of the following songs of the scale five times.
Can you play with correct rhythm by the fifth time?

Repeat five times, carefully keeping the rhythm.

No.1

No.2 Keep the rhythm

No.3 Pay attention to the rhythm

No..4 Pay attention to the rhythm

No.5 Keep the rhythm

No.6

Auld Lang Syne

Scottish Air

Hark the Herald Angels Sing!

Mendelssohn

My Old Kentucky Home

Poco Adagio

Foster

Play keeping the rhythm. Play through five times. Can you play smoothly by the fifth time?

Write down how many times you played before you could accurately play:_____times.

Take Volume I (Suzuki Violin), and play Bach Minuets I, II, and III, looking at the music. You must look at the notes. Looking at the notes while keeping the rhythm is an important point in reading. If you play with shaky rhythm, you have no reading ability yet.

Reading Exercises

Play with precise rhythm.

Old Folks at Home

G Major

Foster

64

The second finger on A goes half a step higher. Put 2 close to 3.

Home, Sweet Home

Quietly and beautifully

Bishop

Little Sandman

Poco Animato

German Folk Song

(Don't forget the rhythm.)

The Blue-bells of Scotland

Andante (two beats)

Scottish Air

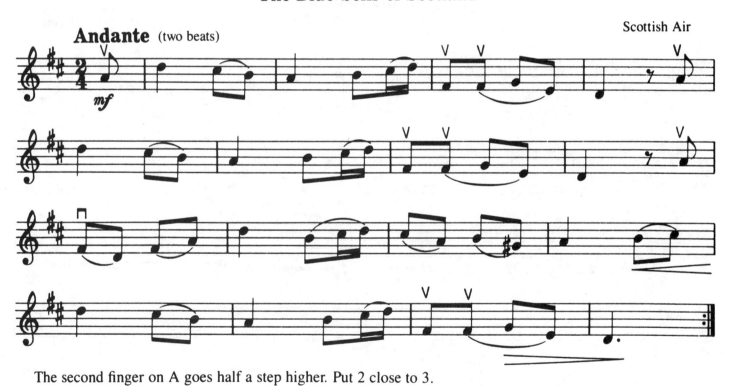

The second finger on A goes half a step higher. Put 2 close to 3.

On a Journey

Moderato Semplice

J. P. Ordway

I have omitted finger numbers.
Test yourself to see how well you can play without numbers.

Annie Laurie

Lady John Scott

Try playing while keeping the rhythm.

Next, try playing the Handel Bourrée
(Volume 2) looking at the music. See if
you can now play with the music a little
more easily than before.

Die Lorelei

Andante

Fr. Silcher

rhythm

1 2 3 4 5 6   1 2 3 4 5 6

dim. . . . . . . gradually softer

Old Black Joe

Poco Adagio is a solemn and slow piece. For convenience's sake, count eight per measure when you play this type of music.

rhythm   1 2 3 4 2 2 3 4   1 2 3 4 2 2 3 4

Poco Adagio

Foster

allarg. (slowing down)

F Major

Play five times in a row.

Cuckoo

German Folk Song

Oh Susanna

Foster

When you don't understand the finger position or finger number, refer to the finger pattern table in Part IV of this book.

Free as a Bird

Spanish Melody

This is in d minor.

Play this piece at about the tempo of a healthy person's pulse.
a tempo: at the tempo of the beginning
rit.: gradually slower
dim.: gradually softer

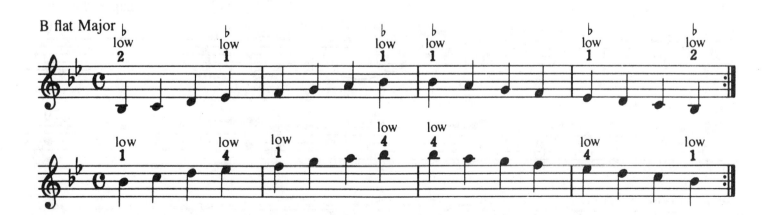

These are the notes with flats. The fingers are low (half a step down).

Zum Sanctus

Slowly—this is a song of prayer.

Schubert

The Lighthouse Keeper

English Melody

Play Volumes 1 and 2 of Suzuki Violin looking at the music yourself.

Andante

W. A. Mozart

Heidenröslein

Werner

Add dynamics to the following pieces. Just follow the notes.

(dynamics)

Lullaby

Quietly and beautifully

Toyohashi Folk Song

dim. *rit.*

dim. *rit.*

Ruined Cottage of Home

Moderato

W. S. Hays

La Donna e Mobile
from "Rigoletto"

Verdi

3/8 — Three beats, counting an eighth note as one beat.
Play roughly at the waltz tempo. Play spiritedly and light-heartedly.

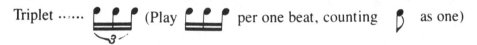

We Are Gathered Together
Summer School Song

Shinichi Suzuki

When a natural is attached to a note after a flat has been added, it means that the note goes back to the original tone. Whenever there is a natural, think that the note has gone back to the note in the C Major scale.

Part VI

Table of Fingering Patterns

Third Position

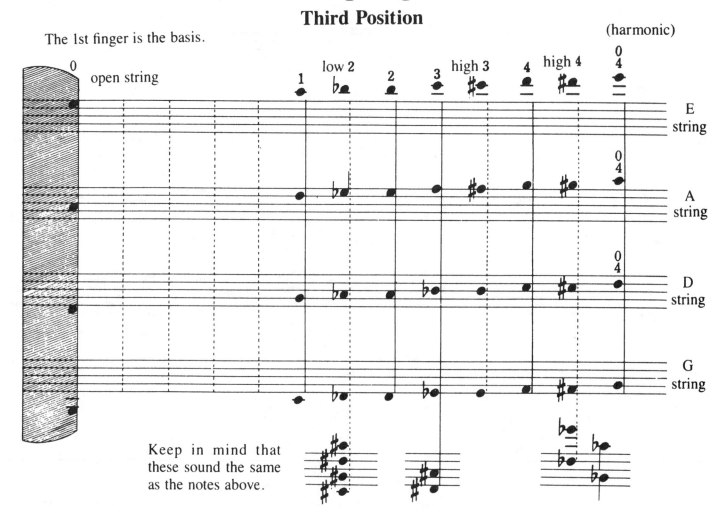

The 1st finger is the basis.

Keep in mind that these sound the same as the notes above.

Third Position

When you play in third position, the first finger falls where the third finger would normally be in first position. The finger pattern would be established from this position. The first finger note is a fourth above the open string.

This table should prove helpful to those who are studying *Position Etudes*.

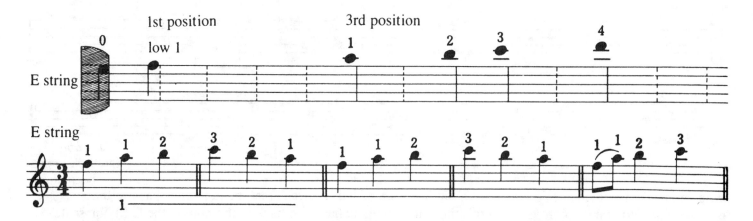

Repeat each measure five times. Read the finger numbers.

Repeat each measure five times. Say the finger numbers aloud.

Securely learn the fingers above in the 3rd position on the four strings. If you know these clearly as the basics, the rest will simply be an application of this.

In order that you will comprehend the above with greater clarity and absorb it, I add the following exercises. As usual, you should practice until you can say a finger number for one pulse.

Reading Exercises
Third Position

Exercise 1

Repeat each measure five times.
After you practice saying the numbers, write them down.

Whether a note has a flat, a natural or a sharp, the finger number is the same. It is just a matter of whether the note is half a step high or low, etc.

Exercise 2 (over all the strings)

After saying the finger numbers five times, write in the numbers in the 3rd position. Whether there is a sharp or not, the finger number is the same. The sharp only means that it is half a step higher.

Exercise 3

First repeat each measure five times, staying in third position, then write, saying the numbers aloud.

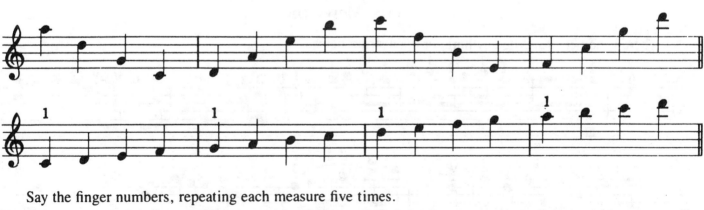

Say the finger numbers, repeating each measure five times.

Exercise 4

Practice understanding which position it is in. Repeat each measure three times.

Write I for the 1st position

Write II for the 2nd position   under the notes.   I recommend using a red pencil.

Write III for the 3rd position

When the same position continues, write   I ----- II ----- III ----

Concerto in A Minor
First Movement

There is no need to write anything for open string notes.

Vivaldi

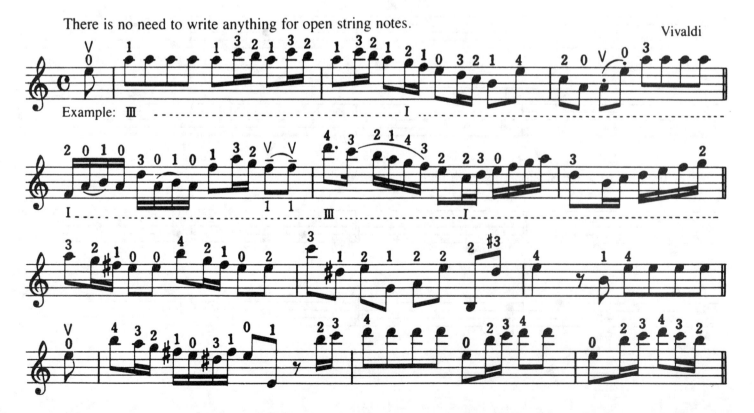

Third Movement

Concerto for Two Violins
Second Violin

Bach

Exercise 5

This time, let's do the opposite: I will show positions I, II, and III, and ask you to write in finger numbers. Study the example carefully.

Example:

Menuet

Write in fingers according to the position instruction.

Bach

The rest is omitted.

If you have any questions, refer to the table of finger patterns given at the beginning.

Gavotte

J. Becker

Exercise 6

Test your ability. Write both finger numbers for each note: the 1st position number under the note, and the 3rd position number above the note. See how much time it takes.

Example:

Test yourself with Long, Long Ago quoted below.

        The 1st position --------- how many seconds?
        The 3rd position --------- how many seconds?

Try it. If the difference between the two is big, you should study the 3rd position more thoroughly.
Remember to write the 3rd position fingers on top, and 1st position fingers below.

Achievement test   I should take less than 60 seconds (how much can you reduce the time?)
                     III should take less than 60 seconds (how much can you reduce the time?)

If it takes more than 60 seconds, repeat practicing. It means insufficient
practice. Study the first pages of this book solidly.

New World Symphony

Dvořák

The rest is omitted.

In this piece,   I should be finished within 90 seconds (how much faster than 90 seconds?)
             III should take less than 90 seconds (how much faster than 90 seconds?)

Allegro Melody

Achievement Test Time   Can you write each within 30 seconds?

Twinkle Melody

Achievement Test Time   Can you write each in 15 seconds?

Go Tell Aunt Rhody

Achievement Test Time   Can you write each in 30 seconds?

If you cannot finish within the designated time, erase and try again. I recommend using a light pencil.

First, Second and Third Position
A and D Strings

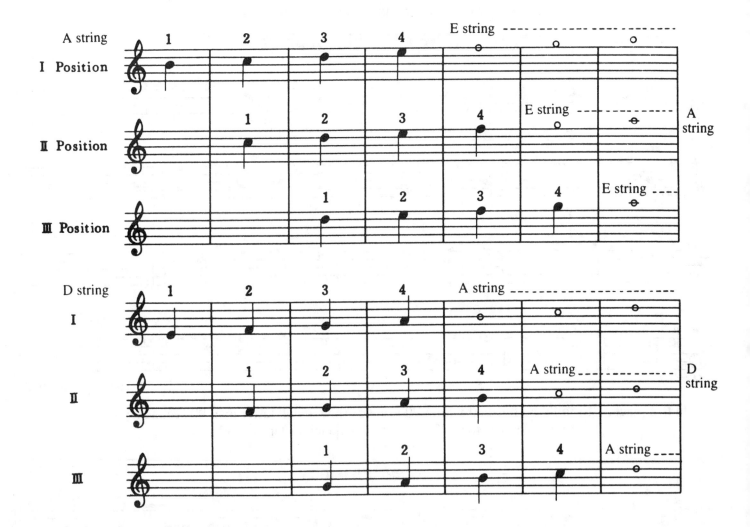

Repeat each measure 3 times in 10 seconds.
Say the fingers in each position.

You cannot pass the section if it takes more than 10 seconds to do a measure three times.

First, Second, and Third Position
E and G Strings

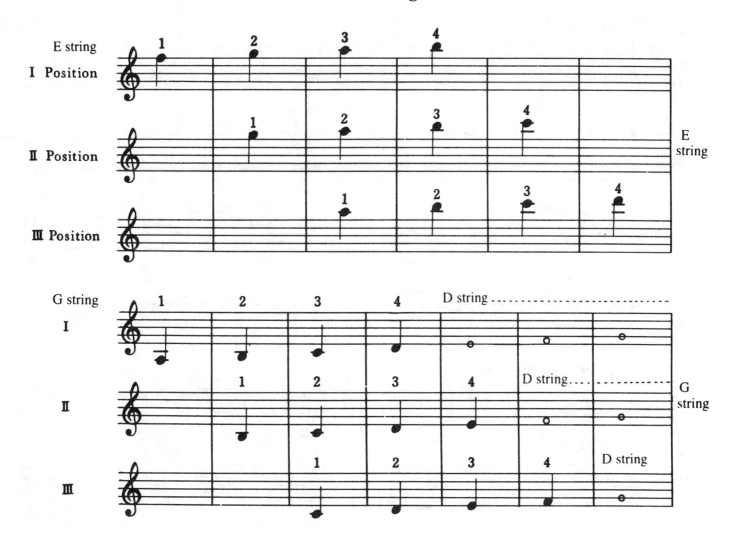

Say each measure 3 times in 10 seconds
Say finger numbers quickly in each position.

86

Write in finger numbers.

La Folia

Adagio

Corelli

When you finish writing in finger numbers, practice thinking about the lengths of notes while keeping the rhythm.

German Dance

Dittersdorf

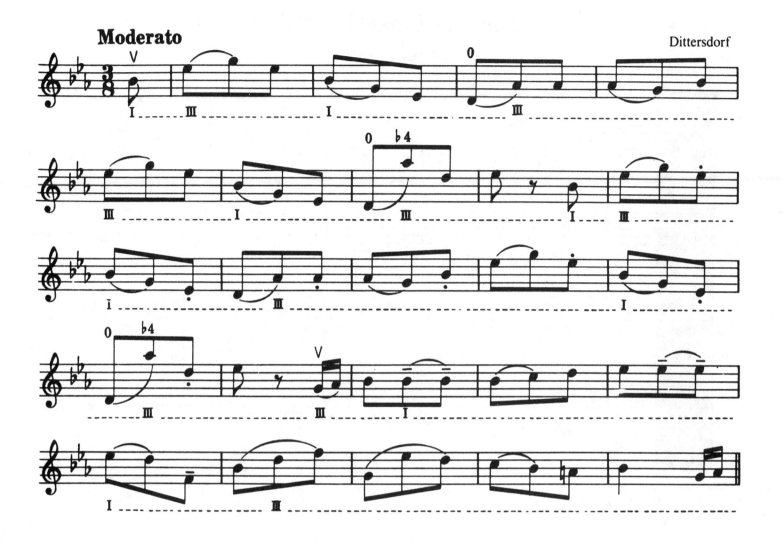

Exercise 1   Write in fingers.

Exercise 2   Add a flat to each of the flat notes. (First carefully examine the notes below.)

The following octave notes also have a flat.

Part VII

Table of Fingering Patterns

Fourth Position

As shown in the table, in the 4th position, the place of the 4th finger in the 1st position is taken by the 1st finger, and from there the fingers 2, 3, and 4 are determined. Therefore, the 1st finger needs to be trained as the basic finger until a secure, intuitive sense of position develops. The following notes are played by the first finger:

Even if a sharp or a flat is attached, it is still the same finger in the same position.

(See *Position Etudes*)

Position

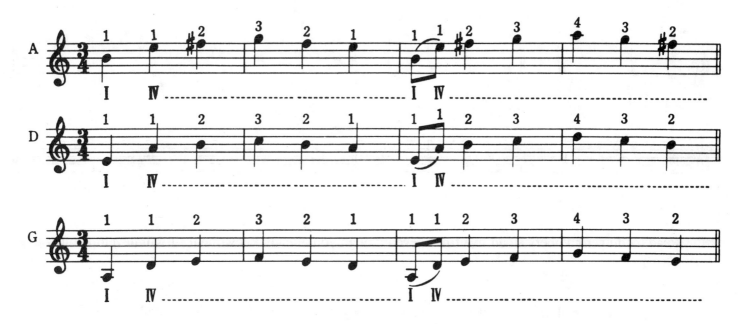

Write in finger numbers (after saying them five times).

Write in finger numbers (after saying them five times).

Read the finger numbers aloud five times, even though you already know them. It will develop your ability.

The weakness of modern people is that they possess knowledge without ability.
Many understand, but few digest the knowledge required to develop a real ability.
"I understand, I understand," we may say; but when we try in earnest, we find
that we cannot do it as well as we thought.
What have I done in my life? When we reflect upon ourselves, many find they
have done nothing. I am among the rest.
All our lives, we say, I understand, I understand, and so many live without
achievement. (These are words of self reflection quoted from my diary.)

Mark positions I, II, III, IV under the following staffs.

Concerto in G Minor
Third Movement

The following is for reference. Take a careful look at changes in positions. If you notice them on the spot, it means that ability has been developing in you. You can congratulate yourself.

(Volume 5) Vivaldi

※ means that I want you to pay attention.

After you glance through the whole example, write in the positions I, II, III, IV.

Table of Fingering Patterns
Fifth Position

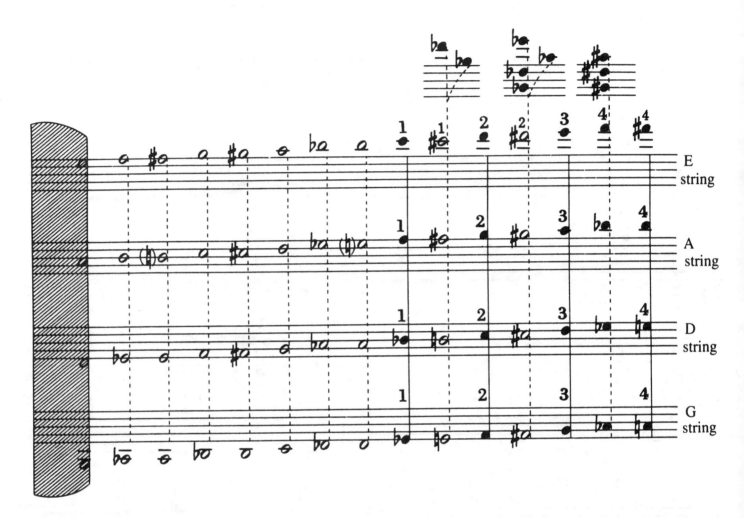

In the 5th position, as shown in the table above, the 1st finger plays a fifth higher than the 1st finger in the 1st position.

Look at the other strings except for the E string. It is one string down from the 1st position, the fingers being the same. Therefore, the 1st and 5th positions are distinguished by indicating the string when it is in the 5th position:

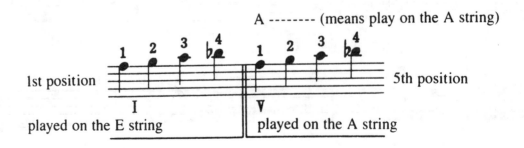

Hence, just think that the 5th position fingers are identical to the 1st position fingers in relation with the notes, except that the strings are one string lower. Remember this.

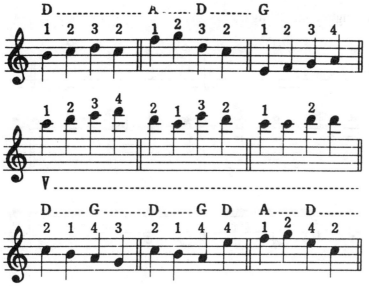

Write in.
Don't forget which string.

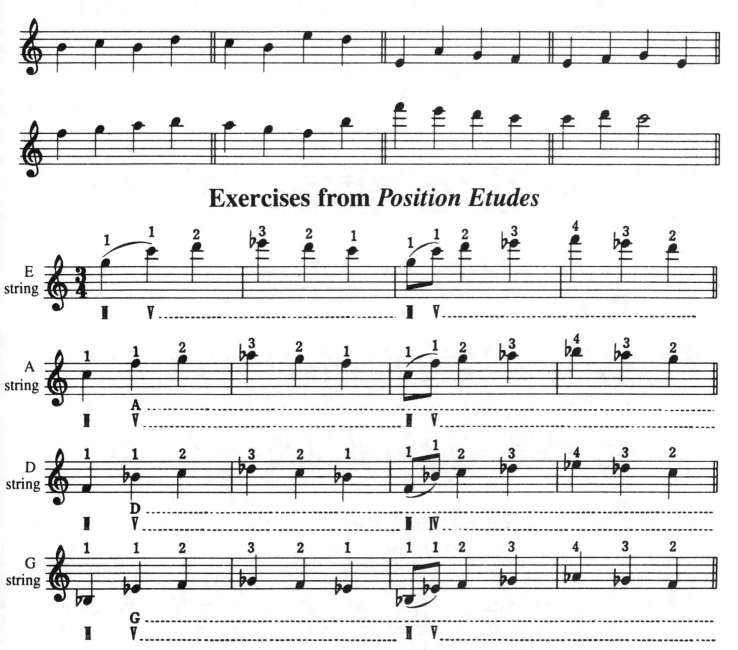

Exercises from *Position Etudes*

94

Which string?　　Write in fingers and strings.　　　　　　　　　　5th Position

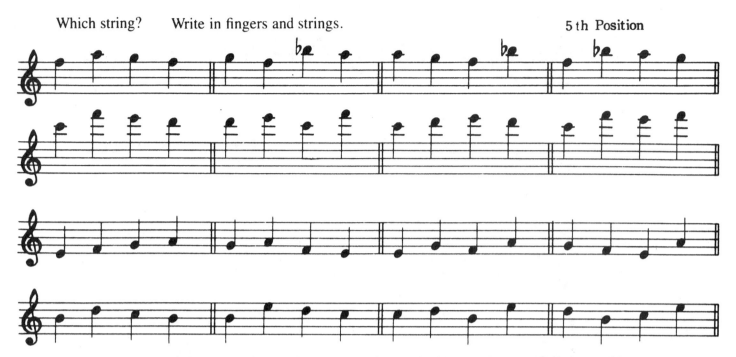

When you don't understand the intonation, play in the 1st position and compare the sounds.

Concerto in A Minor
Second Movement

Write in finger numbers. Count eight beats per measure.
(Volume 5)

Vivaldi

Concerto in G Minor
First Movement

(Volume 5)
³indicates triplet.

Vivaldi

The Sixth and Seventh Positions

About these positions, let me just quote examples from *Position Etudes* for reference's sake. The first five positions are used most often, and they will suffice up to Suzuki Violin Volume 8. Since I think you already understand the meaning of positions, I am sure you will understand the 6th and 7th positions as the need arises.

Sixth Position

96

In many cases, it says in the music "G ----" with finger numbers written in. It does not indicate a position such as "VI ----." That is because it is enough to indicate the finger number on G; there is no need to say that it is in the 6th position.

Seventh Position

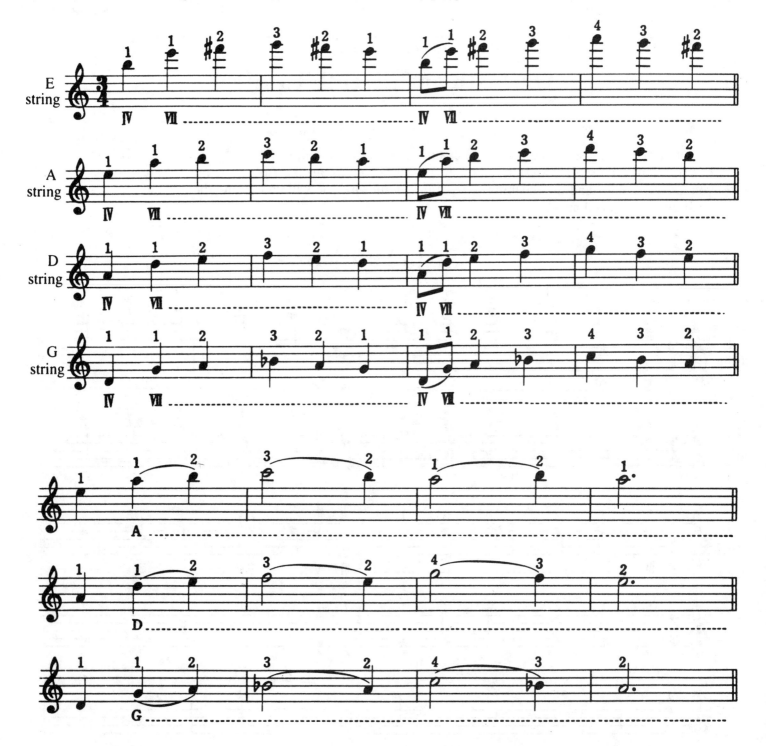

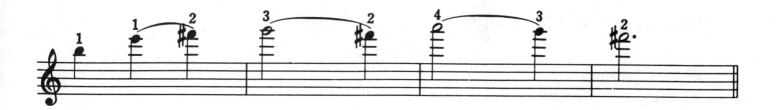

We have generally finished going over problems of positions. As a result of your daily efforts with your children, you have been developing in yourselves important musical abilities. You have become more discerning in recognizing a beautiful piece, and the quality of nobility, in finding it moving; you can hear wrong intonation, and distinguish between fine and unskillful performances. The combination of these elements constitutes musical power. While fostering your children, you are nurturing an important ability in yourselves.

Comprehensive Review

Let me give you some problems here so that you can test how much you have absorbed what you have been studying. If there is anything you cannot do, go back to the pertinent sections of this book and study once again. If you can answer all the problems, you can say that you now read music. The numbers refer to the parts of this book.

Exercise I

Write finger numbers in the 1st position.

Is the 2nd finger in this piece high 2 or low 2?

Write out the beat in fractions:  

Gavotte

Exercise 2 (a minor)

Write in finger numbers (1st position). Mark open string notes with O.

Lully

The rest is omitted.

Gavotte

Exercise 3

Mozart

Write in the 1st position numbers to this beautiful gavotte, and ask your child to play it in $\frac{2}{2}$ meter, counting two beats per measure, using the fingering you have written. It is fine if you sing it yourself, too, but be careful about the rhythm. If the fingers are wrong, it will turn out to be an awful melody.

Try the same with the following Waltz by Brahms.

Waltz

After writing in the fingers, try reading note names.
(Part III)
Rhythm: this is a slow waltz.

Tambourin

Exercise 4

Write in fingers

Rameau

Allegro moderato

Country Dance

Exercise 5

Write in fingers

Weber

Allegretto

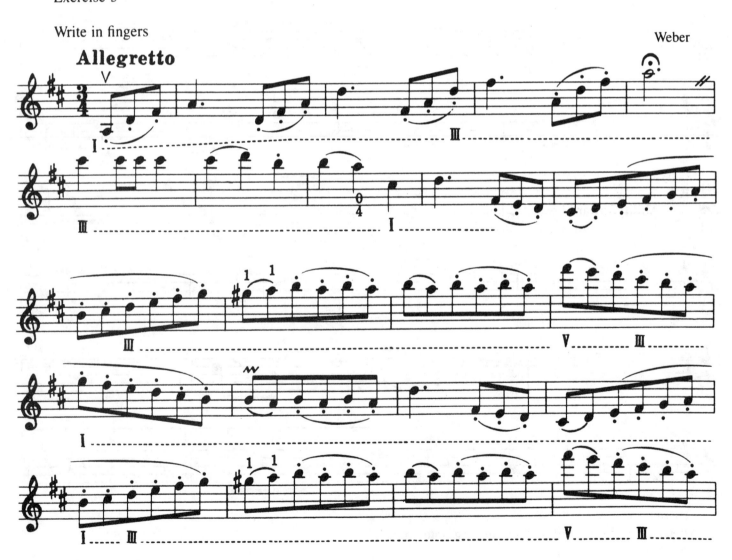

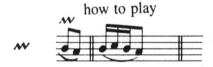

how to play

An Immediate Goal

Only children who practice with an immediate goal in the next step will progress.
Progress means that ability develops toward the next step.

Ability toward beautiful tone;

ability toward precise intonation;

ability to express correct and proper rhythm.

Practice every day more than a minute or two using a single note so that, in time, you will be able to produce a beautiful and fine tone.

Two examples:

Pay attention to intonation and practice *slowly,* improving it.
Are you doing what is natural—feeding music through the ear by playing the Suzuki Violin records for your child? What a big difference there is when a child listens to the records. This is a characteristic teaching method in talent education.
After your child has learned a piece, are you helping him to achieve more accurate and musical rhythm?

Part VIII

Those who are studing *Position Etudes* should play the pieces below.
Students who have studied the first to the third positions in *Position Etudes* should be able to play them. Test your ability up to Mendelssohn's "Spring Song."

The following pieces are a level above Suzuki Violin Volume 4.

Serenade

Andante cantabile

J. Haydn

★ Written:

Played:

This is played　　　　　this way.

Calando   dim.

Berceuse Slave

F. Nerúda

Serenade

Moderato

Schubert

This is a triplet. Do not forget to keep the $\frac{3}{4}$ rhythm of the piece.

Don't rush. Play three notes fully and richly.

Spring Song

Allegretto grazioso

F. Mendelssohn

The following pieces are a level above Suzuki Violin Volume 6.

Danse Espagnole

Andantino quasi Allegretto

E. Granados

110

Chant Hindou

Andantino

Rimsky Korsakow

poco rall.